STUD

Discover
HEBREWS

by
Elizabeth Vander Haagen

FAITH
ALIVE®
Christian Resources

Grand Rapids, Michigan

*In these last days [God] has spoken to us by his Son,
whom he appointed heir of all things, and through whom
he made the universe. The Son is the radiance of God's
glory and the exact representation of his being,
sustaining all things by his powerful word.*

Hebrews 1:2-3

*Through Jesus, therefore, let us continually offer to God
a sacrifice of praise—the fruit of lips that confess his
name. And do not forget to do good and to share with
others, for with such sacrifices God is pleased.*

Hebrews 13:15-16

Unless otherwise noted, Scripture quotations in this publication are from
the HOLY BIBLE, NEW INTERNATIONAL VERSION, © 1973, 1978, 1984,
International Bible Society. Used by permission of Zondervan Bible
Publishers.

Cover photo: SuperStock

We welcome your comments. Call us at 1-800-333-8300 or e-mail us at
editors@faithaliveresources.org.

ISBN 978-1-59255-287-0

5 4 3

Contents

How to Study

The questions in this study booklet will help you discover for yourself what the Bible says. This is inductive Bible study—in which you will discover the message for yourself.

Questions are the key to inductive Bible study. Through questions you search for the writers' thoughts and ideas. The questions in this booklet are designed to help you in your quest for answers. You can and should ask your own questions too. The Bible comes alive with meaning for many people as they discover the exciting truths it contains. Our hope and prayer is that this booklet will help the Bible come alive for you.

The questions in this study are designed to be used with the New International Version of the Bible, but other translations can also be used.

Step 1. Read each Bible passage several times. Allow the ideas to sink in. Think about their meaning. Ask questions about the passage.

Step 2. Answer the questions, drawing your answers from the passage. Remember that the purpose of the study is to discover what the Bible says. Write your answers in your own words. If you use Bible study aids such as commentaries or Bible handbooks, do so only after completing your own personal study.

Step 3. Apply the Bible's message to your own life. Ask,

- What is this passage saying to me?
- How does it challenge me? Comfort me? Encourage me?
- Is there a promise I should claim? A warning I should heed?
- For what can I give thanks?

If you sense God speaking to you in some way, respond to God in a personal prayer.

Step 4. Share your thoughts with someone else if possible. This will be easiest if you are part of a Bible study group that meets regularly to share discoveries and discuss questions.

If you would like to learn of a study group in your area or would like information on training to start a small group Bible study,

- call toll-free 1-888-644-0814, e-mail smallgroups@crcna.org, or visit www.FaithAliveResources.org/DYB.

Introduction

The book of Hebrews is unique; its style is distinct from that of other letters in the New Testament. It reads more like a sermon than a letter, taking the form of a carefully constructed argument based on many Old Testament passages. In this way Hebrews is similar to the teaching of a Jewish rabbi in a synagogue on the Sabbath.

Though we don't know who wrote Hebrews or exactly whom it was written to, it's clear that the book was written to believers in Jesus who had become exhausted. They were tired of being Christians, tired of suffering for their faith, and tired of waiting for Jesus to come back. In their burned-out state they were in danger of drifting in their journey with God. So the writer, or preacher, of Hebrews aims to encourage these believers to hold on, in God's strength, by refocusing on the author and founder of their faith—the Lord Jesus Christ.

This "back to basics" book outlines who Jesus is and why faith in him matters, and it focuses particularly on Jesus as our high priest and our "once for all" sacrifice (Heb. 10:10-12). Assuming an audience that's familiar with the Old Testament, Hebrews is a "word of exhortation" (Heb. 13:22), urging its first readers to continue living faithfully for their Savior, Lord, and King.

Hebrews also speaks to us today, reminding us of all that Jesus is and all he has done for us, encouraging us to live faithfully in times when we too may be weary and in spiritual danger.

Glossary of Terms

Aaron—the brother of Moses; in the law given to Moses after the Israelites' release from slavery in Egypt, God instructed Aaron (from the tribe of Levi) to be high priest and his sons and other descendants of Levi (Levites) to be priests for God's people Israel (Ex. 28-29; Lev. 8-9).

Abel—son of Adam and Eve; he was killed by his brother, Cain (Gen. 4).

Abraham—the father of the Israelite nation whom God called to follow him in faith. God promised to bless "all peoples on earth" through Abraham (Gen. 12:3). Jesus ultimately fulfilled that promise by making God's salvation possible for people of all nations. Abraham is also called the father of all believers (Rom. 4:11-12; see Gal. 3:29).

altar—an altar is a place where sacrifices are made; animals and incense were burned on altars as offerings to God in Old Testament worship (see Gen. 8:20; 12:8; Ex. 27:1-8; 30:1-10).

angels—supernatural beings created by God to be messengers, to carry out God's will in this world, and to serve and care for all who belong to God (Ps. 91:11-12).

apostle—"one who is sent." God sent Jesus into this world to bring salvation from sin for all who believe (Luke 4:18-19; John 6:38-40; Heb. 3:1).

ark of the covenant—a wooden chest overlaid with gold and placed in the Most Holy Place in the tabernacle. It symbolized the presence of God among the people of Israel (Ex. 25:10-22). See also **atonement cover**. Inside the ark were the stone tablets of the Ten Commandments (Ex. 34:1-28), a jar of manna, and Aaron's staff—all reminders of God's provision and covenant with the people.

atonement—reconciliation; the gracious work of Christ that brings sinners into a right relationship with God (1 John 2:1-2).

atonement cover—a cover of pure gold placed on the top of the ark of the covenant. The cover served as a kind of throne where God met with Moses and gave him all the commands for the Israelites (Ex. 25:20-22).

burnt offerings for sin—When the people of Israel sinned, intentionally or unintentionally, they were to make a burnt offering to atone for (pay for) their sins. For these offerings, animals without defect were killed and burned on the altar (Lev. 4-6). See also **Day of Atonement**.

Cain—firstborn son of Adam and Eve. Cain killed his brother, Abel, because God accepted Abel's sacrifice and not Cain's (Gen. 4).

ceremonially unclean—in a state of religious impurity, according to Old Testament law. This condition could be corrected by performing certain rituals and sacrifices (Lev. 10:10-11).

cherubim—winged creatures often described in Scripture as attending God's throne in heaven. God instructed Moses to place two carvings of cherubim on the cover of the ark of the covenant (see Ex. 25:17-22).

Christ—see **Messiah**.

consecrated bread—twelve loaves of bread placed on a gold table in the tabernacle (Lev. 24:5-8). Representing the twelve tribes of Israel, the loaves reminded the people that God would provide for them.

covenant—a binding and solemn agreement; God made covenants with Noah (Gen. 9:8-17), Abraham (Gen. 15, 17), and the people of Israel at Mount Sinai (Ex. 19-24). In Jesus Christ God makes a new covenant with us, promising us forgiveness and the power to live in a way that pleases the Lord (Luke 22:20; Heb. 8). Jesus fulfilled the old covenant (old testament) in every way and established the new covenant (new testament) through his "once for all" sacrifice to save us from sin and death (Heb. 10:10-18).

curtain—see **tabernacle**.

Day of Atonement—annual day of rest, fasting, and sacrifices to cleanse the Old Testament people of their sins (Lev. 16). On this day the high priest was allowed to enter the Most Holy Place in the tabernacle to present before God the sacrifice for the sins of all the people.

Enoch—a faithful believer who "walked with God" and did not die "because God took him away" (Gen. 5:22, 24; Heb. 11:5).

Esau—Along with his twin brother, Jacob, Esau was a son of Isaac, the son of Abraham. Esau was older than Jacob, but he sold his right of inheritance to Jacob for some stew when he was hungry (Gen. 25:29-34).

eternal life—life that lasts forever with God. It begins when one receives Jesus by faith as Savior (John 6:40), and it reaches fulfillment in the new heaven and earth when the believer's soul is reunited with his or her resurrected body to live in God's presence forever (1 Cor. 15:20-54).

exhortation—to exhort is to urge passionately; an exhortation is a speech or writing given to urge an important point or teaching. The book of Hebrews is an exhortation—it's more like a sermon than a letter, it is based on many Old Testament passages, and it features a style of discussion similar to that used by a Jewish rabbi in the synagogue on the Sabbath. Hebrews was written to urge believers to hold on to their faith.

faith—"Faith is being sure of what we hope for and certain of what we do not see" (Heb. 11:1). Faith is confidence in the word and promises of God, even when what is promised is unseen. Through faith in Jesus Christ we are made right with God (Rom. 3:22).

glory—splendor, majesty, power, worth, excellence of quality and character. In the Old Testament God's glory was represented in a cloud (Ex. 33:12-34:7). God's glory is also revealed in the world around us (Ps. 19:1). Jesus revealed God's glory through his teaching and miracles and through his death and resurrection (John 2:11; 11:4; 12:23-28). In Christ, we also reflect God's glory (2 Cor. 3:18).

God the Father—the first person of the Trinity. The other two persons are God the Son (Jesus Christ) and God the Holy Spirit. They are three persons in one being.

gospel—This word literally means "good news" and refers to the message of God's salvation from sin and the promise of eternal life through Jesus Christ. This word can also refer to one of the first four books of the New Testament (Matthew, Mark, Luke, and John) that tell the good news story about Jesus.

grace—God's undeserved favor and forgiving love. Jesus is the full expression of God's grace for the salvation and new life of all who believe in him as Lord and Savior (Eph. 2:8-10).

heifer—a young cow, often used for sacrifice in the Old Testament (Num. 19:1-8).

high priest—The high priest represents God to the people and the people to God. There were many priests in Israel who served at the tabernacle and later at the temple making offerings and leading worship. The high priest would make the offering for all of the sins of the people on the Day of Atonement (see Ex. 28-29; Lev. 16; Num. 18; Deut. 31:9-13).

holy—perfect in goodness, purity, and righteousness (Eph. 4:22-24).

Holy Place—See **tabernacle.**

Holy Spirit—the third person of the Trinity. The other two persons are God the Father and God the Son (Jesus Christ). They are three persons in one being. The Holy Spirit convicts us of sin, works true faith in our hearts, and empowers us to live holy lives. The Spirit's presence in our hearts guarantees that we will receive God's promises (John 16:7-15).

hope—in combination with faith this means looking ahead in solid trust to the fulfillment of all God's promises (Heb. 7:19; 11:1).

house of Israel, house of Judah—during the history of the Israelites the nation of Israel split into two kingdoms, one called Israel and the other called Judah (1 Kings 12).

hyssop—a plant used for sprinkling blood and water for cleansing (see Lev. 14:49-53; Ps. 51:7; Heb. 9:19).

inner sanctuary—the place where God dwells, symbolized by the Most Holy Place in the tabernacle (Lev. 16:2).

Isaac—the promised son of Abraham and Sarah (Gen. 17:19; 18:1-15; 21:1-7). God tested the faith of Abraham by telling him to sacrifice Isaac to the Lord; Abraham obeyed, but Isaac was delivered at the last minute when an angel of God called Abraham to stop (22:1-19).

Israel, Israelites—the descendants of Abraham, Isaac, and Jacob (whom God renamed Israel—Gen. 32:28). The Israelites were God's chosen people (Deut. 7:6).

Jacob—Along with his twin brother, Esau, Jacob was a son of Isaac, the son of Abraham. God renamed him Israel (Gen. 32:28), and he had twelve sons whose descendants became the nation of Israel (Gen. 27-35).

Jerusalem—the ancient city once known as Salem, when Melchizedek was its king (Gen. 14:18). It later became the capital of Israel under King David (2 Sam. 5:4-10). David's son Solomon built the temple of the Lord there (1 Kings 6-8), and in Jesus' day it was again the religious center for God's people. Jesus suffered there and was crucified outside the city walls (Luke 23:26-33; Heb. 13:12).

Joshua—successor to Moses as leader of the Israelites. Joshua led the people into the promised land of Canaan, but because of their disobedience the people never truly found rest there (Judg. 2:6-23; Heb. 4:8).

Judah—the son of Jacob from whom Jesus descended (Matt. 1:3; Heb. 7:14).

lampstand—a pedestal of seven lamps placed in the Holy Place of the tabernacle. God commanded that the lamps be kept burning every night (Ex. 25:31-40; 27:20-21).

law—refers to the body of Old Testament writings prescribing the law that God gave to the Israelites for daily living, summed up in the Ten Commandments (Ex. 20; see also Matt. 22:37-40).

manna—a food that God provided for the Israelites during their travels in the desert after their release from slavery in Egypt. The manna appeared on the ground each morning, except on the Sabbath, and could be used for baking bread (see Ex. 16; John 6:32-35).

mediator—a person who brings about reconciliation between two parties. Under the new covenant, Jesus Christ is the supreme mediator between God and sinful people (1 Tim. 2:5). See also **high priest**.

Melchizedek—a historical figure mentioned in Genesis and considered a model pointing to Jesus Christ. Because there is no record of Melchizedek's parents or children (no known beginning or end to his life), he symbolizes the eternal nature of Jesus. Because he was a priest of God apart from the Levites, he symbolizes the priesthood of Christ, which is not of the Levitical priesthood. Because he was both a priest and king, he symbolizes the royal priesthood of Christ, who is both priest and ruler of the kingdom of God. (See Gen. 14:17-20; Ps. 110:4.)

mercy—a term often used to describe kindness and compassion to someone in distress. To be more precise, it refers to showing leniency by holding back punishment even if justice calls for it (see Mic. 7:18-19).

Messiah—the promised deliverer of God's people. Both the Hebrew word *Messiah* and the Greek word *Christ* mean "Anointed One." Through the prophets God promised to send the Messiah to deliver God's people from their oppressors and to rule them in righteousness forever. The people misunderstood these promises, however, and looked for a Messiah who would be a political ruler and gather an army to rout all their physical enemies. But as Jesus revealed through his work and teaching, the Messiah came to save God's people from the oppression of sin and death and to give them new life forever with God. As King, Jesus Christ rules today in heaven at the right hand of the Father, and when he comes again at the end of time he will fully establish God's everlasting kingdom of righteousness on earth. (See Matt. 26:63-64; John 16:5-16; 1 Cor. 15; Rev. 21:1-5; 22:1-5.)

Moses—the leader of the Israelites when God delivered them from slavery in Egypt and as they lived in the wilderness before entering the promised land (Canaan). Moses received the law from God and taught it to the Israelites.

Most Holy Place—see **tabernacle.**

Noah—builder of the ark in which God saved his family and land animals from the great flood (Gen. 6-9).

oath—a sworn solemn pledge in which a person calls on someone greater (such as God) as a witness. God also makes oaths (Ex. 33:1; Ps. 110:4). An oath is used "to put an end to all argument" or speculation about the fulfillment of a promise (Heb. 6:17).

Passover—This feast took place each spring to celebrate the Israelites' exodus from slavery in Egypt. The name commemorates God's protection of Israelite households during a final plague sent to convince the Egyptian king (pharaoh) to let the Israelites go. God promised that upon seeing the blood of a sacrificed lamb on the doorframes of a house, God would *pass over* that house and not allow the plague of death to take the life of the firstborn in that house (see Ex. 12).

perfect, perfection—complete, finished; see also **holy.**

priests—officials who served in the temple and belonged to the tribe of Levi; also often called Levites. See also **high priest**.

prophet—someone God chooses to speak God's message (Deut. 18:17-19).

purification—removal of any uncleanness or sin; in the Old Testament purification was sometimes done with ceremonial washing or sprinkling and sometimes with burnt offerings. Jesus purified us, or made us clean and holy, through his death (Heb. 1:3; 1 John 1:7).

redemption—the condition of being freed from captivity by payment of a ransom. Jesus Christ paid the penalty of sin by his death to save sinners who otherwise would die under the law's punishment (Rom. 3:23-24).

repentance—the word *repent* means "turn around" or "turn back"; repentance for sin involves turning around one's life to live for God as Lord and Savior (Luke 5:32; 2 Cor. 7:10).

rest—in Hebrews the word *rest* often refers to a promised end of hardship and struggle, a state in which people can flourish in peace and righteousness in the presence of God. God promised the Israelites rest in the promised land (Canaan) as a pointer to eternal rest in the new heaven and earth, but they often did not have rest because they disobeyed God and violated the covenant (Judg. 2:6-23). In Scripture, rest is also associated with the Sabbath—the day set apart by God in the Old Testament for rest and worship (Ex. 20:8).

righteousness—the condition of being right with God; righteousness has to do with right relationships, with responding to God and others in ways that are just. As God's people, we are called to be righteous and are given Christ's righteousness: we are made right with God through Christ's death and given the ability to live in right relationships with others through the power of the Holy Spirit (Rom. 3:21-26).

Sabbath—the seventh day of the week, set apart as a day of rest and worship according to the law of Moses. Jewish religious leaders developed a stringent code of rules for keeping the Sabbath, and Jesus often criticized them for being too legalistic in this regard (see Mark 2:23-3:6; Luke 13:10-17; John 5:16-17; 7:21-24). See also **rest**.

sacrifice—an offering given to God to regain right standing with God. In the Old Testament (old covenant), right standing was regained by offering an animal sacrifice for sin. To establish the new covenant, Christ offered himself as the "once for all" perfect sacrifice for the sins of all who believe in him (Heb. 10:10).

salvation—eternal deliverance from the power and penalty of sin; salvation is possible only through the finished work of Jesus Christ, in whom we believe as Savior and Lord (John 3:16; 14:6).

sanctify—to make holy. Sanctification is the process of spiritual growth by which the believer learns to live more and more in a way that honors Christ (2 Cor. 3:18).

Sarah—wife of Abraham and mother of Isaac; she was long past childbearing age when she gave birth to Isaac (Gen. 18:1-15; 21:1-7).

sin—disobedience to God; refers to breaking God's law (1 John 3:4).

Son of God—this title for Jesus describes his relationship with God the Father as part of the Trinity. God the Father, God the Son, and God the Holy Spirit are three persons in one being.

Son of Man—Jesus used this term to describe his humanity as well as to refer to a title associated with the Messiah as described by the prophet Daniel (see Dan. 7:13-14; Matt. 24:30; 25:31; 26:64).

Spirit—see **Holy Spirit**.

tabernacle—the sacred tent that served as the Israelites' place of worship and as a reminder of God's presence among the people. The tabernacle was divided into two parts: the Holy Place and the Most Holy Place. The Holy Place contained a table with consecrated bread, a golden lampstand, and an altar of incense. The Most Holy Place, separated from the Holy Place by a curtain, contained the ark of the covenant. Only the high priest could enter the Most Holy Place—and then only once a year on the Day of Atonement (Ex. 26; Lev. 16:2). King Solomon of Israel replaced the tabernacle with a permanent temple for the Lord in Jerusalem, basing it on the design of the tabernacle (1 Kings 6-8).

throne of grace—this term refers to the atonement cover on the ark of the covenant (where God came to meet with the people—Ex. 25:17-22) and to God's throne in heaven, which we can approach with confidence because of the work of Jesus, our ultimate high priest (Heb. 4:14-16; 10:19-22).

Word (of God)—the true and living message of God (Heb. 4:12); this term is used in the Bible to refer (1) to God's spoken word in creation (Gen. 1) and through prophets like Moses (Ex. 19-24); (2) to God's written Word, the Scriptures (Matt. 5:17; 22:40; 2 Tim. 3:14-17); and (3) to Jesus Christ as the Word of God who "became flesh and made his dwelling among us" (John 1:14).

Lesson 1
Hebrews 1

Jesus Is the Last Word

Additional Related Scriptures

Genesis 1:2-3, 6, 9, 14, 20, 24, 26
Deuteronomy 18:18-22
Psalm 2:7; 19:1; 45:6-7
Isaiah 61:1-3
Malachi 3:6
Matthew 3:13-17; 4:17, 23; 6:9-10;
    17:1-5
Luke 4:16-21
John 8:12, 31-36; 10:28; 14:15-17,
    25-26; 16:7-15

Acts 1:9-11; 2:33-36
Romans 8:17
2 Corinthians 3:18; 5:17-21
Galatians 3:26-4:7
Ephesians 1:18-23
Colossians 1:10-17
Hebrews 10:1-18
James 1:17

Introductory Notes

The first chapter of Hebrews addresses a question that becomes a major theme in the book. "Who is Jesus?" people ask, and the opening words of Hebrews make clear that Jesus is the Son of God the Father. Jesus is the "appointed heir of all things," and through him God "made the universe" (Heb. 1:2). Hebrews 1 also speaks of the Son as the last word, God's final way of communicating with us. Earlier God spoke to our ancestors "through the prophets . . . but in these last days he has spoken to us by his Son" (1:1-2). Jesus is the ultimate Word of God to a world racked with sin and beaten down by all the effects of sin. Jesus is the final answer for every sinner in need of a Savior. As the writer of Hebrews adds later, Jesus is "the author of [our] salvation" (2:10; see 12:2).

In this first chapter of Hebrews we also find a style of discussion that will continue throughout the book: the use of numerous Old Testament Scriptures to illustrate who Jesus is and how Jesus is superior to all.

1. *Hebrews 1:1-3*

    a.   How has God spoken in history?

b. How has God spoken to us?

c. What do we learn about the Son?

d. What has the Son done?

2. *Hebrews 1:4-7*
   a. What is the relationship of the Son to the angels?

   b. What are angels for? What do they exist to do? (See also Heb. 1:14.)

3. Hebrews 1:8-14

a.   What lasts forever? What is changeless?

b.   What is God's kingdom?

c.   What is righteousness? What does it mean that "righteousness will be the scepter of your kingdom" (Heb. 1:8)?

d.   Why do you think the author emphasizes God's changelessness?

e.   What does it mean to make one's enemies a footstool?

Why is it important that Jesus is the last Word about sin and death?

Since Jesus is the exact representation of God's being and we are his followers, can we too be God's representatives? Explain.

How do you feel about the idea that angels are sent to serve those who will inherit salvation? Have you thought of angels that way before?

Lesson 2
Hebrews 2

Listen to Jesus, Our Brother

Additional Related Scriptures

Genesis 1:26-29; 2:15; 3:17-19
Deuteronomy 33:2
Psalm 8:4-6
Daniel 7:13-14
Matthew 4:1-11; 9:6; 19:28; 24:30;
     25:31, 34; 26:64
Luke 19:10; 24:25-27, 44-49
John 1:12-13; 3:16; 10:30; 14:11
Acts 7:38, 53
Romans 5:10-11, 12-21; 6:4-11; 8:34;
     12:6-8

1 Corinthians 1:7; 6:2-3; 10:13;
     12:4-11, 27-31; 13:9-12; 15:3-8,
     20-28
2 Corinthians 5:18-19
Galatians 3:19; 5:22-25
Philippians 2:6-11
1 Timothy 2:4
2 Timothy 2:12
2 Peter 1:16; 3:8-9
1 John 1:1; 3:2-3
Revelation 20:4-6; 22:5

Introductory Notes

Hebrews 2 helps us answer the question "Who is Jesus?" by focusing on Jesus' place as a fellow human being, our brother. This chapter continues the style of discussion begun in Hebrews 1, drawing on passages from the Old Testament, including a quote from Psalm 22, the psalm Jesus prayed on the cross (see Matt 27:46).

Note also that Hebrews 2 begins by urging readers and listeners to pay attention. This call for careful attention comes up again and again in the book of Hebrews, urging us not to lose touch with the amazing gift of salvation we have in Christ.

1. *Hebrews 2:1-4*

   a.   Why do we need to pay careful attention to what we've heard?

b. How was salvation confirmed to the readers of Hebrews?

c. How has salvation been confirmed to you? What signs or testimonies of salvation have you seen or heard?

2. *Hebrews 2:5-9*

Having given the first of many warnings to pay attention, the preacher of Hebrews returns to the earlier discussion of Jesus as greater than the angels (Heb. 1:4-4, 13-14) and having an everlasting kingdom (1:3, 8-13).

a. For whom has Jesus done his work?

b. Why is Jesus crowned with glory and honor?

c. If Jesus has authority over all things, why do we "not see everything subject to him" (Heb. 2:8)?

d. How did Jesus taste death for everyone?

3. *Hebrews 2:10-13*

a. How did God bring many sons and daughters to glory?

b. How could Jesus be made perfect through suffering?

c. Why is Jesus not ashamed to call us his brothers and sisters?

4. *Hebrews 2:14-18*

    a.   Why did Jesus share our humanity?

    b.   Why did he have to be like us in every way?

Questions for Reflection

Often we think of how Jesus had to be God in order to rescue us from sin. How does it feel to know that Jesus also had to be human, like us in every way, in order to save us?

How might this chapter of Hebrews encourage us when we suffer? When we are tempted?

How might this passage help us explain God's love for us as we share the good news of Jesus with others?

Lesson 3
Hebrews 3:1-4:13

Hold On

Additional Related Scriptures

Genesis 2:2-3, 15
Exodus 20:8-11
Numbers 12:6-8; 13-14
Psalm 95
John 1:12; 6:39; 10:28-29; 14:15-17,
    26-27; 15:1-17; 16:7-15
Romans 8:9-17, 26-27
2 Corinthians 1:21-22; 3:17-18;
    5:16-21

Galatians 5:25
Ephesians 1:11-14; 2:19
Philippians 4:7
2 Timothy 3:16-17
Hebrews 2:9-13
1 Peter 2:5

Introductory Notes

In Hebrews 3:1-4:13 the writer compares Jesus to Moses and Joshua, important figures in Israel's history. The author urges readers to "hold on" (3:6), reminding them of the Israelites' experience of wandering in the desert and entering the promised land of Canaan.

Through Moses, God led the people out of Egypt into the wilderness and up to the edge of Canaan. Twelve spies went ahead to see what the land was like—and when they came back, the spies gave different reports. Ten of the spies reported that although the land was wonderful, the people living there were giants and would wipe out the Israelites. The other two spies, Joshua and Caleb, reported that the land was wonderful and the people were fierce but that God would give them victory. The Israelites chose to listen to the ten fearful spies, and, in anger at their disobedience and unfaithfulness, God sent the people back into the wilderness to wander for forty years, until a whole generation died (see Num. 13-14; Ps. 95).

In this way the author of Hebrews argues that Jesus is a greater leader than Moses and that the consequences of turning away from the living God are even greater for Christians than they were for the Israelites.

1. *Hebrews 3:1-6*

    a.   Why is Jesus worthy of greater honor than Moses?

b. How are we God's house?

2. *Hebrews 3:7-4:2*

In verses 7-11, 15 the writer uses quotations from Psalm 95 to urge readers not to turn away from their relationship with God in Christ. Warnings about the danger of falling away occur several times in the book of Hebrews.

The question of whether a believer can fall away, or lose the promise of eternal life, is one that Christians have wrestled with for centuries. In the Reformed tradition we believe you cannot lose your salvation, and we base this teaching on passages such as John 6:39; 10:28-29; 2 Corinthians 1:21-22; Ephesians 1:11-14; and many others. Nonetheless, all Christians are tempted at times to stop trusting, to stop believing in the promises of God. And all Christians are called to be faithful in their relationship with Jesus and to persevere in faith and obedience.

The purpose of these warnings in Hebrews is not to make a theological statement about whether it is possible to lose salvation. Instead, the writer wants to urge believers to stay faithful, to be active in living for Jesus out of thanks for all he has done to save us.

a. Why should we encourage one another daily?

b. Why were the Israelites not able to enter God's rest?

c. In what way was God's message of no value to them?

d. What warning does the writer of Hebrews pass along to us?

e. How can we keep our hearts from becoming hardened? How can we keep from following the example of the Israelites?

3. *Hebrews 4:3-11*
    a. What is the benefit of entering God's rest?

    b. How do we enter this rest?

4. *Hebrews 4:12-14*

a. What does the Word of God do?

b. In this section about holding on, why do you think the writer of Hebrews closes with these comments about the Word of God?

Questions for Reflection

How might looking forward to entering God's rest give you strength when you are weary?

Is the fact that "nothing in all creation is hidden from God's sight" frightening or comforting? Explain.

As you look back on the blessings or benefits mentioned in the passage for this lesson, how would you describe those to someone else?

Lesson 4

Hebrews 4:14-6:20

"Be Greatly Encouraged"

Additional Related Scriptures

Genesis 12:1-5; 14:18-20; 15:1-21;
   17:15-22; 21:1-7; 22:15-18
Exodus 40
Leviticus 16
Psalm 2:7; 31:5; 66:18; 110:4
Isaiah 59:1-2
Matthew 4:1-11; 6:33; 13:1-23;
   26:36-45; 28:19-20
Mark 1:4
Luke 1:37; 4:1-13; 22:39-46; 22:63-
   23:43; 24:25-27

John 5:24; 8:44; 9:31; 14:15-17, 25-26;
   19:30
Acts 1:9-11; 6:1-7; 19:1-7
Romans 8:34; 12:1-2
2 Corinthians 5:17, 21
Philippians 2:5-8
2 Timothy 2:11-12
Hebrews 2:17-18; 4:15-16; 7:3;
   9:24-25; 12:2
James 4:3

Introductory Notes

In our Scripture for this lesson the writer of Hebrews identifies Jesus as our great high priest. Priests played an essential role in the relationship between God and the Israelites in the Old Testament. The first priest of God mentioned in the Bible was Melchizedek (Gen. 14:18-20), who lived even before the time of the Israelites. (We'll learn more about him in lesson 5.)

When God gave the people of Israel his law for holy living, God appointed Moses' brother Aaron to be their high priest. Once a year Aaron, and every high priest after him, would go into the Most Holy Place in the tabernacle (and later in the temple—1 Kings 6-8) to present an offering (atonement) for the sin of the people. The Most Holy Place, where the ark of the covenant was kept, was a symbol of God's presence and dwelling among the people (Ex. 40; Lev. 16).

Once again the author of Hebrews uses passages and stories from the Old Testament to urge readers to hold on to their faith and trust in God, because Jesus as our priest understands us and God is faithful.

1. *Hebrews 4:14-5:9*

    a.   Why should we hold firmly to the faith we profess?

b. What does a high priest do? How is the high priest chosen?

c. How did Jesus become our high priest? Why was he chosen?

d. What do we read here about Jesus' prayers? How might this encourage us in our journey of faith?

e. What does it mean that Jesus was "made perfect"?

f. What does it mean to be "in the order of Melchizedek"?

2. **Hebrews 5:11-6:12**

    a.   What does the writer of Hebrews mean by "milk" and "solid food"?

    b.   Is it impossible to repent if you have fallen away?

    c.   Why do we need to show diligence to the very end?

3. **Hebrews 6:13-20**

In this closing section of Hebrews 6, the writer reassures us that God can be trusted. God promised Abraham, who was childless, that he would have many descendants. Twenty-five years later, God gave Abraham and his wife Sarah a son, Isaac. From Isaac and his descendants came all of the people of Israel. In addition, God promised to bless Abraham and his descendants and to give them the land of Canaan; God also promised that Abraham's descendants would be a blessing to all nations (Gen. 12:1-5; 15:1-21; 17:15-22; 21:1-7; 22:15-18). That promise is fulfilled in Jesus Christ.

    a.   Why did God make an oath to Abraham?

b.   In what ways can we be greatly encouraged?

Questions for Reflection

How do you hold on to faith? How do you keep from slipping away? What is the anchor that secures you?

In this lesson what have you learned about Jesus as our high priest?

Do you approach God with confidence? Explain.

Lesson 5
Hebrews 7

Jesus and Melchizedek

Additional Related Scriptures

Genesis 14; 18:16-33
Exodus 28-29; 32:11-14
Numbers 6:22-27; 18:1-32; 23:21
Deuteronomy 18:1-2
2 Samuel 5:4-10
Psalm 110
Isaiah 9:6
Micah 6:6-8

Mark 12:30-31
Luke 11:42
John 1:1-5, 10-15
Romans 8:26, 34, 39
2 Corinthians 9:6-11
Hebrews 6:16-20
1 John 2:1-2

Introductory Notes

Hebrews 7 continues to describe Jesus as our great high priest by comparing him with Melchizedek and Aaron, two significant high priests in the Old Testament, as noted in lesson 4. There is no explanation of where Melchizedek came from or how he came to be a priest (see Gen. 14:18-20). In the law given to Moses after delivering the people of Israel from Egypt, God instructed Aaron (from the tribe of Levi) to be high priest and his sons as well as other descendants of Levi (Levites) to be priests (Ex. 28-29). Priests offered prayers and sacrifices on the people's behalf, and they brought God's blessing to the people (see Numbers 6:22-27 and 18:1-32 for more information on the duties of priests).

1. *Hebrews 7:1-3*

    a. What is unusual about Melchizedek?

    b. How is Melchizedek like the Son of God?

c.   What's significant about Melchizedek's name and title?

2.   *Hebrews 7:4-10*
    a.   Is Melchizedek greater than Abraham? Explain.

    b.   What did the law require of the descendants of Levi who became priests?

3.   *Hebrews 7:11-22*
    a.   Was the Levitical priesthood perfect? Explain.

    b.   On what basis did Jesus become a high priest?

c.   What is the better hope that Jesus' priesthood introduces?

4. *Hebrews 7:23-28*
   a.   Why is Jesus the guarantee of a better covenant?

   b.   What is so important about the oath?

   c.   What does it mean to intercede for someone?

   d.   How does Jesus' priesthood benefit us?

Questions for Reflection

How might thinking of Jesus' kingship and priesthood enrich your understanding of him? Your relationship with him?

Why is it significant that Jesus sacrificed for our sins "once for all"? How does this show he is our ultimate high priest? What does it mean for our relationship with God?

Lesson 6
Hebrews 8-9

High Priest of a New Covenant

Additional Related Scriptures

Exodus 19-31; 34:1-28; 40
Leviticus 4; 10:1-2; 16; 26:12
Numbers 4; 15:22-29
1 Kings 6-8
Psalm 14:1-3; 103:12
Ecclesiastes 7:20
Isaiah 43:25; 53:6
Jeremiah 7:23; 31:31-34
Ezekiel 11:20
Zechariah 8:8
Matthew 5:17-48; 15:19-20; 26:28;
    27:51

Mark 14:24
Luke 22:20
John 8:34
Acts 1:9-11; 5:31; 13:38-39
Romans 3:10-12; 7:14-25; 8:18-25
1 Corinthians 13:8-12
2 Corinthians 3:18
Ephesians 1:7
Philippians 2:13; 3:20-21
Titus 2:11-14
Hebrews 4:16; 9:15
Revelation 4; 5:9

Introductory Notes

In Hebrews 8-9 the writer continues to use examples from the history of Israel to address the question "Who is Jesus?" Jesus is our high priest, and not only that—he is the high priest of a new covenant, changing worship and our relationship with God forever.

These chapters compare the new covenant that God makes with us in Jesus Christ to the old covenant that God made with the people of Israel through Moses (Ex. 19-24). God promised to be the people's God and commanded them to obey his law. This law included the Ten Commandments and many instructions for holy living and worship. Part of the law had to do with priests and sacrifices and setting up the tabernacle. The tabernacle (and later the temple—1 Kings 6-8) was the place where God lived on earth, where God came to be present among the people (Ex. 40). The people of Israel would worship at the tabernacle and bring their sacrifices to be offered there. God also gave specific instructions about building the tabernacle and about conducting worship and sacrifices (Ex. 25-31).

Because Jesus is the high priest of a new covenant, we are completely cleansed of our sins and no longer separated from God. We are forgiven, and we have a new, intimate relationship with God. We can "approach the throne of grace with confidence" (Heb. 4:16), bringing our needs, our concerns for others, and our worship into God's presence.

1. *Hebrews 8:1-6*

   a.   Where does Jesus serve as our high priest?

   b.   How is Jesus' ministry superior to that of other priests?

2. *Hebrews 8:7-13*

   a.   Why do we need a new covenant?

   b.   What does God promise in the new covenant?

3. *Hebrews 9:1-10*

   a.   How was the earthly tabernacle set up?

b. How could priests on earth enter the Most Holy Place?

c. What was the Holy Spirit showing by all this?

4. *Hebrews 9:11-15*

a. How did Jesus enter the Most Holy Place?

b. How are our consciences cleansed, and what are the results?

5. *Hebrews 9:16-28*

a. How is a covenant like a will?

b. How did Jesus' finished work put the new covenant into effect?

c. How did Christ do away with sin?

d. What will Christ do when he appears a second time?

Questions for Reflection

When you think about your relationship with God as a covenant, does that change your impression of the relationship? Explain.

Does the idea of Jesus being a priest in heaven seem strange? Comforting? Confusing? Explain.

In what ways do you think this lesson can help you explain the importance of Jesus' work to others?

Lesson 7
Hebrews 10

Jesus' Sacrifice and Our Response

Additional Related Scriptures

Leviticus 17:11
Psalm 110
Jeremiah 31:34
Matthew 24:36-42
John 6:38-40; 8:28-29

Romans 6:23; 8:1-4
Philippians 2:6-11
Colossians 2:15
Hebrews 1:3, 13; 2:1, 13; 3:12;
    4:15-16; 5:6; 6:4-6; 8:10; 11:1

Introductory Notes

Our Scripture for this lesson weaves together two themes we have already seen in the book of Hebrews: the priesthood of Jesus and the call to hold on. The writer-preacher continues to compare worship in the earthly tabernacle (as regulated by the law of Moses) to the worship that is now possible because of Jesus Christ. In this chapter the writer draws again from the Old Testament to show how Jesus' sacrificial death makes us holy, and in this assurance we can "hold unswervingly to the hope we profess," knowing that "he who promised is faithful" (Heb. 10:23).

To be made holy is to be set apart and purified. Holiness is one of the unique characteristics of God, and God requires it of his people so that they can live in his presence. When God gave the law to the people through Moses, God called the people of Israel to be a holy nation by obeying the law. When the people sinned, sacrifices were made so that they could be cleansed from their sins and become holy again. Jesus' sacrifice cleanses us and makes us holy "once for all" so that we can persevere as God's people in this world.

1. *Hebrews 10:1-4*

    a.   Could the law make worshipers perfect? Why?

b. What were sacrifices an annual reminder of? Why?

2. *Hebrews 10:5-18*

   a. What did Jesus do according to God's will?

   b. How have we been made holy?

   c. Where is Jesus now? What is he waiting for?

3. *Hebrews 10:19-25*

   a. What gives us the confidence to enter into God's presence?

b.   How are we to respond to Jesus and the living way he has opened for us?

4.   *Hebrews 10:26-31*

In this section we find another warning against falling away. As noted in earlier lessons (see 2:1; 3:12; 6:4-6), the preacher of Hebrews is not concerned with the theological question of whether a person can lose salvation; instead the writer is concerned with the urgency of holding on to faith. The sin referred to in verse 26 is apostasy—the sin of publicly rejecting Jesus Christ. Apart from Christ there is no sacrifice that can cover sin, and there is only judgment.

a.   What happened to those who rejected the law of Moses?

b.   What will happen to those who, having known Jesus and tasted his goodness, reject him?

5.   *Hebrews 10:32-39*

a.   How did the Hebrew believers respond to earlier experiences of suffering?

b.   Why did these believers need to persevere?

Questions for Reflection

What benefits do you see in your life as a result of Jesus' "once for all" sacrifice?

In what ways can it be helpful to look back on earlier times in your life when you've suffered? In what ways do you see that God cared for you and perhaps strengthened or shaped your faith?

Lesson 8
Hebrews 11-12

Living by Faith

Additional Related Scriptures

Genesis 4:1-16; 5:18-24; 6-9; 12-17;
    22:1-18
Exodus 2:1-15:31; 19:10-25
Matthew 28:20
John 1:14; 3:16; 14:26; 16:13-16

Romans 8:18-25, 28; 12:1
1 Corinthians 3:11-15; 12:9, 31-13:13
Hebrews 4:9-11
2 Peter 2:5
Revelation 21:1-4

Introductory Notes

Hebrews 11 and 12 are about faith and faithfulness. The writer of Hebrews begins by defining faith (11:1) and reminding readers about important stories of faith, stories of "the ancients"—believers from long ago who lived by faith over the long haul. These believers are examples of faith, and they point to Jesus, who in addition to being our high priest is also the author and perfecter of our faith.

In these two lengthy chapters the writer wrestles with the question "Why is life so hard?" To help believers formulate answers in their own context, the writer points back to other faithful believers who endured hardship, points to Jesus who helps us live by faith, and points ahead to the Lord's coming kingdom, in which "there will be no more death or mourning or crying or pain" (Rev. 21:4).

1. *Hebrews 11:1-6*

Hebrews 11 lists and refers to many stories from the Old Testament. Although we will touch on some of those stories in this lesson, you may still have a variety of questions. The *NIV Study Bible* is particularly helpful with this chapter, giving references and explanations about the many stories.

    a.   What is faith? What do we understand by faith?

b. What are some of the things people did by faith?

c. What makes it possible for us to please God?

2. *Hebrews 11:7-16*
    a. What did Noah do?

    b. What was Abraham looking for?

    c. How did "all these people" manage to live by faith until they died,
        especially when they hadn't fully received what was promised?

3. **Hebrews 11:17-31**

    a.   How does Abraham's sacrifice point to Jesus?

    b.   How was Moses a role model for the readers of Hebrews?

4. **Hebrews 11:32-40**

    a.   What did faith empower believers to do, as mentioned in these verses?

    b.   Why didn't any of these people fully receive what was promised?

5. **Hebrews 12:1-3**

    a.   In response to the stories of faith in Hebrews 11, what are we to do?

b.   Why are we to consider Jesus?

6.   *Hebrews 12:4-13*

In these verses the preacher of Hebrews is not saying that all suffering and hardship are sent by God to discipline us; nor is the writer suggesting we should seek ways to suffer so that we may become disciplined. Instead we need simply to recognize that pain and suffering are part of the human experience in this world and that God can use suffering and hardship for our good.

a.   How are we to think of hardship?

b.   Why does God sometimes discipline us?

7.   *Hebrews 12:14-29*

a.   Why are we to make every effort to be holy?

b. Having received "a kingdom that cannot be shaken" (Heb. 12:28), what is a fitting response?

Questions for Reflection

Do you feel that you've received what God has promised? Explain.

How do you respond when life is hard? How does it affect your relationship with God?

Lesson 9
Hebrews 13

Instructions for Faithful Living

Additional Related Scriptures

Genesis 18:1-19:13
Exodus 22:21
Judges 6:11-24
Matthew 5:43-48; 25:35, 40
Luke 22:32
John 10:14-18; 21:15-17
Acts 16:1-3; 17:14-15; 19:22
Romans 8:26-27, 34
Galatians 5:22-25

Ephesians 6:21-24
Philippians 4:12-13
1 Thessalonians 5:25-28
1 Timothy 1:16; 4:11-16
Hebrews 4:16; 7:2; 10:8-10, 19-22;
    11:10, 16
1 Peter 2:25; 5:4, 12-14
3 John 13-14

Introductory Notes

The book of Hebrews ends as many New Testament letters do, with concrete instructions about faithful living and a few personal details from the author. Although Hebrews ends this way, it is mainly a "word of exhortation" (13:22), a sermon based on Old Testament passages. In this final chapter we see a summary of some of the book's major themes: Jesus as our high priest, our new access to God and ability to worship God, freedom to live by the new (eternal) covenant now that Christ has fulfilled the old covenant, and God's unchanging faithfulness in Jesus Christ.

This closing section of Hebrews is the final application part of the preacher's sermon, giving believers specific ways to continue in their faith despite exhaustion and discouragement. The book ends with a benediction (a prayer for blessing) and some personal details about the writer's hopes to visit the readers soon.

1. *Hebrews 13:1-8*

   a.   Why should we be hospitable to strangers?

b. How can we be content with what we have?

c. How can we be encouraged in faithful living by remembering our leaders?

2. *Hebrews 13:9-16*
   a. Why did Jesus suffer "outside the city gate" (Heb. 13:12)?

   b. How can we continually offer to God a sacrifice of praise?

3. *Hebrews 13:17-19*
   a. For what reasons are we to obey our leaders?

b. How can we support our leaders?

4. *Hebrews 13:20-25*

   a. What is the writer's final prayer for the readers?

   b. How does the writer close this sermon to the Hebrews?

Questions for Reflection

If you were to give some specific instructions to believers to urge them to hold on to their faith, what would you say?

How does the statement "Jesus Christ is the same yesterday and today and forever" (Heb. 13:8) encourage and comfort you?

What are some of the ways God has been equipping you and working in you?

An Invitation

Listen now to what God is saying to you.

You may be aware of things in your life that keep you from coming near to God. You may have thought of God as someone who is unsympathetic, angry, and punishing. You may feel as if you don't know how to pray or how to come near to God.

"But because of his great love for us, God, who is rich in mercy, made us alive with Christ even when we were dead in transgressions—it is by grace you have been saved" (Eph. 2:4-5). Jesus, God's Son, died on the cross to save us from our sins. It doesn't matter where you come from, what you've done in the past, or what your heritage is. God has been watching over you and caring for you, drawing you closer. "You also were included in Christ when you heard the word of truth, the gospel of your salvation" (Eph. 1:13).

Do you want to receive Jesus as your Savior and Lord? It's as simple as A-B-C:

- **A**dmit that you have sinned and that you need God's forgiveness.
- **B**elieve that God loves you and that Jesus has already paid the price for your sins.
- **C**ommit your life to God in prayer, asking the Lord to forgive your sins, nurture you as his child, and fill you with the Holy Spirit.

Prayer of Commitment

Here is a prayer of commitment recognizing Jesus Christ as Savior. If you long to be in a loving relationship with Jesus, pray this prayer. If you have already committed your life to Jesus, use this prayer for renewal and praise.

Dear God, I come to you simply and honestly to confess that I have sinned, that sin is a part of who I am. And yet I know that you listen to sinners who are truthful before you. So I come with empty hands and heart, asking for forgiveness.

I confess that only through faith in Jesus Christ can I come to you. I confess my need for a Savior, and I thank you, Jesus, for dying on the cross to pay the price for my sins. Father, I ask that you forgive my sins and count me as righteous for Jesus' sake. Remove the guilt that accompanies my sin and bring me into your presence.

Holy Spirit of God, help me to pray, and teach me to live by your Word. Faithful God, help me to serve you faithfully. Make me more like Jesus each day, and help me to share with others the good news of your great salvation. In Jesus' name, Amen.

Bibliography

Bandstra, Andrew. *In the Company of Angels: What the Bible Teaches, What You Need to Know.* Grand Rapids, Mich.: Faith Alive Christian Resources, 1995.

Barker, Kenneth L., et al. *The NIV Study Bible.* Grand Rapids, Mich.: Zondervan, 1985.

Bromily, Geoffrey W. *The International Standard Bible Encyclopedia.* Grand Rapids, Mich.: Eerdmans, 1988.

Bruce, F.F.. *The New International Commentary on the New Testament: The Epistle to the Hebrews, Revised Edition.* Grand Rapids, Mich.: Eerdmans, 1990.

Long, Thomas G. *Interpretation: A Bible Commentary for Teaching and Preaching: Hebrews.* Louisville, Ky.: Westminster John Knox, 1997.

Wright, Nicholas Thomas. *Hebrews for Everyone.* Louisville, Ky.: Westminster John Knox, 2004.

Evaluation Questionnaire

DISCOVER HEBREWS

As you complete this study, please fill out this questionnaire to help us evaluate the effectiveness of our materials. Please be candid. Thank you.

1. Was this a home group ___ or a church-based ___ program? What church?

2. Was the study used for
   ___ a community evangelism group?
   ___ a community faith-nurture group?
   ___ a church Bible study group?

3. How would you rate the materials?

   Study Guide
   ___ excellent ___ very good ___ good ___ fair ___ poor

   Leader Guide
   ___ excellent ___ very good ___ good ___ fair ___ poor

4. What were the strengths?

5. What were the weaknesses?

6. What would you suggest to improve the material?

7. In general, what was the experience of your group?

Your name (optional) _____

Address _____

8. Other comments:

(Please fold, tape, stamp, and mail. Thank you.)

Faith Alive Christian Resources
2850 Kalamazoo Ave. SE
Grand Rapids, MI 49560